D0717373

Columbia University

Contributions to Education

Teachers College Series

No. 881

AMS PRESS

NEW YORK

Some Sources of Children's Science Information

AN INVESTIGATION OF SOURCES OF INFORMATION AND ATTITUDES TOWARD SUCH SOURCES AS USED OR EXPRESSED BY CHILDREN

By *Mary* CATHARINE BERGEN, Ph.D.

TEACHERS COLLEGE, COLUMBIA UNIVERSITY
CONTRIBUTIONS TO EDUCATION, NO. 881

*Published with the Approval of
Professors Gerald S. Craig and Arthur T. Jersild
Co-Sponsors*

BUREAU OF PUBLICATIONS
TEACHERS COLLEGE, COLUMBIA UNIVERSITY
NEW YORK, 1943

Library of Congress Cataloging in Publication Data

Bergen, Catharine Mary, 1912-
    Some sources of children's science information.

    Reprint of the 1943 ed., issued in series: Teachers
College, Columbia University. Contributions to educa-
tion, no. 881.
    Originally presented as the author's thesis, Columbia.
    Bibliography: p.
    1. Science--Study and teaching (Elementary)
2. Learning, Psychology of. 3. Science--Ability
testing. I. Title. II. Series: Columbia University.
Teachers College. Contributions to education, no. 881.
LB1585.B38 1972   372.3'5   71-176689
ISBN 0-404-55881-X

Reprinted by Special Arrangement with Teachers
College Press, New York, New York

From the edition of 1943, New York
First AMS edition published in 1972
Manufactured in the United States

AMS PRESS, INC.
NEW YORK, N. Y.   10003

Acknowledgments

THE author is greatly indebted to her sponsors, Professors Gerald S. Craig and Arthur T. Jersild for guidance and suggestions; and also to Professors Helen M. Walker, S. Ralph Powers, and Herbert J. Arnold for helpful advice.

The study would not have been possible without the cooperation of Dr. Rollo G. Reynolds, Principal, and Dr. Ina Craig Sartorius, Assistant Principal of the Horace Mann School; of Dr. George Hayward, Principal of the Elmwood School in East Orange, New Jersey; and of Mrs. Gertrude Talley, Assistant Principal in the New York City public school system. Miss Dorothy Wheatley of the public schools of East Orange, New Jersey, has also been of assistance in the study.

The author wishes to thank Charles K. Arey as well as her many other fellow students who have contributed their time to this study.

C. M. B.

ACKNOWLEDGMENTS

I am possessed of a study such as this necessitates the assistance and cooperation of a great many persons. Among the many to whom I am deeply indebted, particular thanks are due:

Dr. Arthur I. Gates, co-sponsor, who will understand that my gratitude exceeds my vocabulary.

Dr. Robert L. Thorndike, co-sponsor, who gave friendly encouragement and invaluable assistance at all stages of the research;

Dr. Harold W. McCormick, Director of the Survey of the Study of the Care and Education of the Physically Handicapped in the City of New York, who made necessary administrative arrangements, and gave valuable advice.

The members of the Subcommittee on Readability of the Committee for the Study of the Care and Education of Physically Handicapped Children in the Public Schools of the City of New York, for valuable criticism and suggestions.

The Mergenthaler Linotype Company, for the loan of assorted matrices and other materials.

The A. B. Dick Company, manufacturers of Mimeograph Products, for supplying the stencils and doing the Mimeography necessary in the experiment.

And others too numerous to mention here, who were of real assistance in the conduct of the study.

M. J. METZ.

Contents

CHAPTER I

Introduction

EDUCATIONAL practices are subject to changes from time to time. Such changes reflect the consensus of opinion among those who are actively examining and evaluating the practices. Ideas announced and explained by these persons are, in turn, considered by teachers. When many teachers find the ideas good, they are put into operation.

In his study of the origins and development of elementary school science, Underhill[1] discusses some recent trends in teaching science in the elementary school. He mentions the increasing efforts which teachers are making to provide situations which will give children problem-solving activities. He enumerates instances in which certain recent textbooks on elementary science have stressed the problem-solving point of view. Any attempt at problem solving requires the use of at least one source of information. In cases where the facts necessary for the solution of the problem are already known by the child, the use of a source must have taken place at some time in the past. The facts are then subjected to certain processes of thinking or reasoning until some conclusion is reached. Often the process of reasoning leads to the need for additional facts and a source of information must again be used. There is some reasoning connected with the use and selection of the source of information.

There have been various studies dealing with a type of reasoning of elementary school children, such as that of Deutsche[2] concerning the development of children's concepts of causal relationships. Studies have also been made of the use which chil-

[1] Orra E. Underhill, *The Origins and Development of Elementary School Science.* 1941.
[2] J. M. Deutsche, *The Development of Children's Concepts of Causal Relationships.* 1937.

1

dren make of individual sources of information such as books. Gans[3] studied and tested children's determination of the relevancy and reliability of reading matter for problems under consideration. But as far as the author knows no studies have yet been completed of the sources which children choose under various conditions. For example, no study has purported to show under what circumstances children tend to suggest an empirical source as opposed to an authoritarian source. It was the aim of the present study to investigate sources of information chosen by children when confronted by certain problem situations, especially those in the fields usually designated as science.

The investigation was designed to provide information with respect to several related questions, as follows:

1. What sources of information do children tend to use or suggest in response to various types of problems and what are their attitudes toward such sources?
2. What is the effect of the teacher as far as can be ascertained in determining children's selection of sources of information and attitudes concerning such sources?
3. What sex differences are evident in the children's suggestions of sources of information?
4. What is the relation between sources of information cited and difficulty of problem?

The question concerning sex differences was included because of the investigator's teaching experience in which she found that boys seemed to have more ability than girls have in handling equipment. The investigator wished to determine whether the boys' skill predisposed them to a tendency to select empirical methods of problem solving and whether the girls' apparent lack of skill predisposed them against such methods.

These questions were studied by two main techniques each of which provided information which could not easily have been obtained from the other. The techniques in question were:

[3] Roma Gans, *A Study of Critical Reading Comprehension in the Intermediate Grades*. 1940.

1. Running records[4] of regular classroom sessions.
2. Individual interviews in which children were asked a set of previously selected questions.

During the classroom sessions it was possible to make records of the children's behavior in a more or less natural situation (if a classroom situation can be called natural); and during the interviews it was possible to observe children in situations which could be kept relatively constant for each of many children. Thus, one technique was used to introduce a degree of naturalness into the study; and the other to introduce a degree of constancy. Other supplementary techniques which were used in connection with the two foregoing techniques will be discussed later.

The first technique, that of classroom records, was used with five third grade classes chosen from two different schools comprising a total of 120 children. The individual interviews were held with the same 120 children and in addition with 72 children from a third school. The third school differed from the first two in that no regular science was taught. The 72 children were so selected that 24 were from first grades, 24 from third grades, and 24 from fifth grades. This enabled the investigator to note changes which age might cause in the selection of sources of information. It was important to choose a school in which there was no science program, as such a program might obscure the effects of age. The classroom records were taken in schools where there were science programs since science sessions were considered to be most fruitful with respect to the situations in which children might conceivably have a choice in their selection of sources of information. This does not mean that the various sources of information are not used in the study of subjects other than science. Obviously, the selection of sources of information is important in any field in which there are problems. Science classes were chosen merely as a matter of convenience because in such classes there were frequent problems of an ob-

---

[4] The phrase *Running records* is used in this study to mean those records made by an observer sitting in the classroom and writing down as much as possible of the conversation and incidents in the room.

jective nature which could be handled easily by children and observed by the investigator.

The classroom records provided information in answer to questions 1, 2, and 3 of the study. The individual interviews furnished additional information concerning questions 1, 2, and 3; and all the information available for question 4.

CHAPTER II

Classroom Records

SELECTION OF CLASSES

IN selecting classes for this part of the study, care had to be taken to procure those in which science was taught more or less regularly, for only during the science periods could one be reasonably sure of observing children who were dealing with science problems. The investigator chose classes from two schools, each of which included science in the curricula of many of their classes, but each of which differed considerably in other respects.

Records of what was happening and what was said were made during several regular class sessions of each of five third grade classes, three of which were in one school and two in another. The former school is situated in a large city. It is a private school with a population of rather high intelligence and high socio-economic level. This school is known throughout the report as School Y. School X, in which two classes were observed, is a public school with children of a low socio-economic level and low average intelligence. This school is located in a small city in a district which has a large colored and Italian population. The two classes from School X will be referred to throughout the report as Class A and Class D; the three classes from School Y, as Class B, Class C, and Class E.

Most of the I.Q. ratings from School X clustered near or below 100. In School Y, nearly all I.Q.'s were above average and a majority of them were above 120. All I.Q. values were taken from school records. The Stanford Binet test had been used in School Y; for School X, the I.Q.'s were taken from a group test, the Pintner-Cunningham.

5

There was a special science teacher in each school. Class D from School X had specified science periods at regular intervals. The science teacher was present for many of these periods. Class A from the same school had no science lessons as such, but records were taken during periods when the children were permitted to contribute any information of interest to themselves which they had found in a newspaper or other source. Many of these contributions were concerned with science topics.

TABLE I

Distribution of Periods of Observation among the Five Classes Studied

School	Class	No. of Pupils	No. of Periods Observed	No. of Hours Observed
X	A	27	7	6
Y	B	23	13	$6\frac{1}{2}$
Y	C	18	15	$8\frac{1}{4}$
X	D	30	9	$5\frac{3}{4}$
Y	E	22	10	5
Total		120	54	$31\frac{1}{2}$

Classes B, C, and E from School Y all had regular science classes, with the science teacher usually present. Several of the children of Classes B and C were older than any child in Class E, and some of the children in Class E were younger than any child in Classes B and C.

Of the 120 children enrolled in the five classes that were observed, 59 were boys and 61 girls. Three of the five classes contained an equal number of boys and girls. In each of the other two classes, the girls outnumbered the boys by one.

Each of the three classes in School Y were observed for at least ten half-hour periods. Since the class periods in School X were longer, records were made of a smaller number of class sessions in this school, but each class was observed during at least seven sessions, representing a total of at least five hours in each class. The numbers of periods of observation and the hours involved are given in Table I.

PROCEDURE IN RECORDING THE OBSERVATIONAL DATA

The records were made by the investigator, who used a combination of shorthand and longhand. As much as possible of the entire conversation was written down. When it was not possible to record everything that was said (and this occurred frequently), remarks which were extraneous to the lesson or which seemed of lesser importance were omitted. Statements which mentioned sources of information or attitudes concerning them or which had to do with the design or modification of experiments were considered more valuable for the purposes of this study than any other types of remarks. The responses were not recorded in their entirety, but in as brief a form as possible without sacrificing the essential quality. This means that some articles and pronouns were omitted, and that children's elaborations which the investigator considered repetitious or extraneous in some form were omitted. The name of the child speaking was recorded with his statement. In some cases it was difficult to determine which child was speaking and the remark was then recorded as coming from an unidentified child. The statements of the classroom teacher and of the science teacher were included, but the children's were given precedence when it was difficult to record all.

RELIABILITY OF THE OBSERVATIONAL DATA

A second observer made records simultaneously with the investigator during four half-hour periods. The two observers differed somewhat as to the material recorded but there was considerable overlapping. Slightly over half the remarks recorded by the investigator were also recorded by the second observer. Many of the remarks recorded by the investigator were not mentioned in the records of the second observer at all; and conversely many of the remarks recorded by the second observer were not mentioned by the investigator. This means that the investigator's records were not reliable as *quantitative* records of class proceedings. It was desired to use them for *qualitative* purposes, mainly, however, and for *quantitative* purposes only in a few instances in which the investigator believes the omissions were not biased.[1] In the latter instances the conclusions are stated with reservations. Hence the remarks recorded by both the investigator and the other observer were the only ones considered in the check for reliability. (The reliability in question is that of the phrasing of the remarks. Since they were not recorded verbatim, it is necessary to ascertain whether the investigator's way of writing them resulted in any misinterpretation of the meanings.)

Consequently the remarks common to the records of both the investigator and the second observer were isolated and examined. There were 173 such remarks. Both sets were analyzed by the investigator in the same manner in which all the records were analyzed in connection with the study (see pages 9-13). It was found that many of these remarks were of an extraneous nature or were repetitions and did not give any evidence that could be used in this study. Such remarks were removed from the list until finally there remained only those which had been recorded by both the investigator and the second observer and which gave evidence pertaining to the study (i.e., evidence of the use of sources of information or of attitudes toward such sources). There were 47 of these remarks. It was found that the phrasing of 87 per cent of these 47 remarks was sufficiently close to permit the same later analysis. The disagreement as to phrasing was largely concerned with remarks of teachers. These facts are shown in Table II (page 9). The four periods for these observations are referred to as class session 1, 2, and so on.

In the case of class session 1 the second observer was the secretary of a science professor in a teachers college; in the case of class session 2 the observer was a doctoral candidate specializing in elementary school science; and in class sessions 3 and 4 the observer was a professional stenographer accustomed to taking classroom records. Before entering the classroom, all three of

---

[1] That is, the omissions were biased as to type of remark, but probably not biased as to the sex of the child who made the remark.

TABLE II

Reliability of Simplified Phrasing of Remarks Recorded in the Classroom by Main Investigator (M) and Second Observer (S)

Class Session	Total Recorded by M	No. of Remarks Recorded by both M and S	% of M's Total Remarks Recorded by S	No. of Pertinent Remarks Recorded by both M and S	No. of Pertinent Remarks on Which M and S Disagreed	
					Teacher's	Children's
1..........	73	50	68%	24	1	
2..........	62	24	39	4		1
3..........	97	50	52	2	1	
4..........	85	49	58	17	3	
Total....	317	173		47*	5	1

* Of the 47 remarks recorded by both observers and containing evidence that was pertinent, 87 per cent were phrased so as to give agreement in results when later analyzed.

these observers were somewhat familiar with the type of evidence sought in the investigation.

TREATMENT OF THE OBSERVATIONAL DATA

The material recorded during the class periods was as far as possible analyzed according to individual problem situations. For example, each of the following was considered a single problem situation:

SCIENCE TEACHER: "What does the earthworm have to breathe with? . . . How could we find out?"
CHILD: "Maybe it would help if we saw one."
2ND CHILD goes to get one which is in the room.

In another class, the children had taken a little baking soda and poured two teaspoonfuls of vinegar over it in an effort to get the mixture to effervesce and form carbon dioxide gas. No action was taking place with the mixture they had made:
SCIENCE TEACHER: "Which should we add more of now?"
1ST CHILD: "Vinegar."
2ND CHILD: "We need more soda. We only used two spoons of vinegar the other day and the foam went higher."

The latter was considered a whole problem, although the incident was but a small part of a larger situation concerned with a study of carbon dioxide.

It sometimes happened that in an effort to explain an observed phenomenon, the children would propose hypotheses which they could test experimentally. The testing procedure was considered a separate problem situation—the problem being whether the hypothesis was or was not true. The mere suggesting of the hypothesis by the children was connected with the original situation in which the problem was to explain the observed phenomenon. Thus a child offering such a hypothesis was giving an answer to the problem of one situation and simultaneously setting the problem for another.

When the classroom records had been divided into problem situations, each remark of a child or the teacher was examined to detect any evidences of reference to sources of information. These sources were classified under the following headings: (1) experiment, (2) observation, (3) printed material, and (4) oral material.

Experiment as used in the study means a suggestion that a certain procedure be tried with materials, or simply a general remark, such as "We could try it." Under this heading were classified also references to previous experiments when mention of such experimenting was offered as a source of information. In the second example of problem situations mentioned above, the child's remark, "We need more soda. We only used two spoons of vinegar the other day and the foam went higher," is an illustration of the use of a previous experiment as a source of information. The word *experiment* is obviously not being used here in its scientific meaning of a highly controlled procedure.

Items classified under the heading of *observation* included suggestions that some object be observed, that a museum be visited, or reference to some object which a child had seen. The remark of the child in the first problem situation quoted, "Maybe it would help if we saw one," was classified under this heading.

Another example of observation suggested as a source of

information occurred after a child asked the question, "Do all planets have the same sky?" One of the other children answered by saying, "At the Planetarium they have only one sky."

The classification *printed material* included suggestions that a fact be sought in a book or an encyclopedia or quotations from a book. Newspapers and printed signs were also classified here.

Recollections of remarks of parents or teachers, or suggestions that information be obtained by asking someone, were classified as *oral material*. This would include such statements as, "My father told me why it happened."

The classifications under *observation* and *experiment* were later grouped together as it proved difficult to separate them in some instances. The combined group is referred to as *empirical sources of information*. *Oral inquiry* was mentioned so seldom that it was grouped with *printed material* in a category called *authoritarian sources*.

Each problem was then analyzed for evidence of attitudes[2] concerning:

1. The appropriateness[3] of a source of information.
2. The reliability[4] of a source of information.
3. Statements concerning the desirability of proving, checking, or repeating experiments; and general statements indicating doubt, uncertainty, or caution.

Fifty of the 199 problem situations (an equal number from each of the five classes) were analyzed by a second person. This person had had experience both as a primary classroom teacher and as a research assistant in education.

Eighty-five per cent of the instances of reference to a source of information detected by the investigator were also selected by the second examiner as evidences of reference to the same sources of information. This co-worker was later asked to repeat

[2] In order to avoid relisting these three aspects of the problems each time they are mentioned, throughout the study they are referred to as attitudes.

[3] "Appropriateness" is used to denote the suitability of a source for the information desired.

[4] "Reliability" refers to the likelihood that the source will provide accurate or authentic information.

the analysis of some of the situations where there seemed to be disagreement, reading the children's and teacher's remarks aloud in the presence of the investigator. In this way it was found that some discrepancies were due to the misinterpretations of the investigator's condensed phrasing of some of the statements. After clarification of these, the agreement between the investigator and the co-worker was 90 per cent. Although only one quarter of the situations were included in this sample, they were so chosen that more than one quarter of the investigator's selections were involved. The co-worker proved to be less exacting in his standards than the investigator and selected some remarks which in the investigator's judgment should not be classed as separate evidence because they involved a repetition of something which the child had said before or because they followed too closely the statement of the teacher or some other child.

Subject-matter statements (as distinguished from statements identifying sources of information or exhibiting any of the attitudes described above), which comprised the largest part of the children's statements, were classified under the heading of *miscellaneous*. This was done to determine the proportion of total remarks made by boys and girls. (All the remarks made in the classroom were not recorded, as explained on page 7, but the investigator can think of no bias which would affect the ratio of boys' remarks to girls' remarks. The omission of some of the remarks was necessitated by the method of recording the data.) According to one of the examiners, 32 per cent of the total remarks (those concerning sources of information or attitudes in addition to those classified as miscellaneous) were made by girls; according to the other only 30 per cent. The co-worker had a large number of remarks for each sex, having classified separately statements which the investigator considered to be repetitions of previous statements. The investigator's analysis for evidence of attitudes toward sources of information was checked by the same co-worker as above. Another set of 50 out of a total of 199 problem situations was examined by the co-worker. Many of the situations contained no evidence which could clearly be interpreted as indicating an attitude on the part of the child. In selecting the 50 situations which were checked by the co-worker, the investigator tended to choose many of those in which she had found evidence that was fruitful in this respect. Actually more than half of these fruitful situations were included in the group of situations that were examined by the co-worker.

Not all attitudes which children exhibited were classified in this study, but only the three stated previously (see page 11). The original analysis involved a greater number, but it was reduced to three as a result of a large disagreement between the investigator and the co-worker with the original set.

There was a 75 per cent agreement between the investigator and the co-worker on the analysis of the 50 situations for statements or actions which could be interpreted as meaning that the child possessed one of the three attitudes. The co-worker classified as attitudes some statements which the investigator considered doubtful.

TEACHERS' REMARKS

The remarks of the classroom teachers and the special science teachers were classified separately. These classifications were not checked by a second examiner for the reason that little use was finally made of them with the exception of those which were categorized in the same attitude group as used for the children.

PROCEDURE FOLLOWING THE CLASSIFICATION OF REMARKS

The remarks classified as sources of information or attitudes were then tabulated and studied with reference to sex, I.Q., class, school, and types of situations in which the remark occurred. Where a relationship seemed possible and interesting the data were grouped to facilitate a determination of chi-square which was tested for statistical significance. In cases where the expected frequencies were less than five and there was a single degree of freedom, Yates's correction for continuity was used.[5] Recombinations of data were effective where there were several degrees of freedom.

Every problem situation containing some remark which was classified in the study as illustrating any of the types of evidence mentioned above (sources of information or attitudes) was then entered on a card—a separate card for each situation. Most of the statements involved in any problem situation were written on the card in red ink; but the one pertinent remark was written in blue ink. When a situation contained more than one pertinent remark it was recopied on one or more additional cards. Only one of the several pertinent remarks was considered on a single card. For example, the following situation was written on two cards:

1st CHILD: "In my opinion, in a book I read called "Science Stories," it said that if the sun were on the earth it would burn the earth up."

2ND CHILD: "If you take a magnifying glass and hold it over paper and burn it (the paper) with the sun's heat, it shows that the sun is hot."

3RD CHILD: "I've tried using it and I saw a boy using it. It burned a spot on a newspaper."

On one card the statement of the second child was in blue ink and on the other the statement of the third child. The first child was merely setting the problem in this case; she was not answering a previous problem but made her remark during a lull in the discussion. There was some doubt whether she believed the book she had read or whether she was questioning it.

ANALYSIS OF CARDS BY SELECTED JUDGES

The cards which contained pertinent references to empirical sources of information or evidences of the attitudes stated above were placed in one pile. The cards pertaining to any one classroom were kept together and arranged chronologically so as to give the reader a better conception of what actually took place

---

[5] R. A. Fisher, *Statistical Methods for Research Workers*, p. 97. 1936.

in a particular classroom. The five groups of cards from the five classrooms were then placed on top of each other in the order of the alphabetical position of the teacher's name, although this order did not seem any more desirable than any other. Those cards which contained pertinent references to books or written materials as a source of information were placed in a second pile.

The investigator then selected five teachers in addition to herself to act as judges in placing the pertinent empirical remarks in categories. These judges were chosen either because they were science teachers or because they were classroom teachers known to be interested in science.

The categories in which the judges were to place the remarks were as follows:

Experiments with some measure of control.
Experiments without the suggestion of control.
Manipulation of materials for the purpose of facilitating observation.
Observation without manipulation but with or without the use of instruments. Visits for the purpose of observation were included.
Attitudes concerning the use of empirical sources of information.

These categories were selected by the investigator in the light of her own analysis of the situations and had been checked by the co-worker as described above before being presented to the judges.

Each category was written on a pink card and the pink cards were sent to the judges with the cards containing the pertinent remarks. Each judge was requested to place each pertinent remark in one of the pink card categories.

In addition, the judges were asked to examine each pertinent remark to see whether it contained any evidence of:

Design of experiment.
Observation.

Theory or interpretation.
Repetition or need of checking.
Control.

Sheets were sent to the judges on which they could indicate their analysis by checking. The judges were given the following directions:

This set of cards contains examples of the suggestions or use of empirical methods as sources of information by third grade children. These examples are written in blue ink. The red ink statements serve to orient the response in its situation. Each card is numbered on the back. The order of numbering depends partly upon the alphabetical order of the teachers' names and partly upon the chronological order of the incidents. You are requested first to take each card in order and analyze the blue ink response for evidence of: design of experiment; observation either in connection with an experiment or otherwise; theory or interpretation; etc. The evidence may be stated in so many words or it may be clearly implied. Indicate your analysis by checking the enclosed sheets which have been prepared for this purpose.

You are asked to sort the cards into piles corresponding to the titles on each of the five pink cards. (Classify only the blue ink statements on each card.) This will facilitate the ranking of the cards as you can rank them separately within each pile. This ranking is to be done according to the quality of the response, putting the highest quality on top of the pile.

Finally place the piles together, putting on top those which indicate the most elaborate empirical methods and so on down to the least elaborate. The pile marked *Attitudes* does not fit into the classification and may be put last of all in the pack. Be sure that each group has its pink card in front of it, so that this card precedes the white cards in its group as you thumb through the pack. Cards which may be classified either in the *Attitudes* group or in one of the other groups should be placed in the other group. Only those cards which do not fit into any other group are to be placed with the attitudes. The attitudes cards are to be ranked according to the degree to which the remarks seem to favor the use of empirical methods for obtaining information.

Some paper clips have been included for your use in clipping together those cards which seem to you to rank exactly the same. Do not use the clips except where it is impossible to detect which of two or more cards is superior.

Kindly avoid writing on any of the cards as they are to be used for other judges.

Please do not consult anyone else in connection with this matter.

Judges for the set of cards containing evidences of empirical sources of information were also given the following definitions:

Design of experiment or technique: Way in which experiment is to be carried out—steps in the procedure.

Observation: What is seen—what one has noticed from personal experience—suggestion that we ought to look for something or watch it.

Theory or interpretation: Statement about the significance of something that is observed during the experiment—conclusions drawn from experiment or some part of it—hypothesis formed in connection with an experiment.

Repetition or need of checking: Repeating experiment or part of it—suggesting that it be repeated—stating that an experiment ought to be performed more than once or that it is possible to make a mistake in doing it the first time—stating that conclusions from experiment ought to be checked with authority.

Control: A method of reducing the variables in an experiment. For example: To test the effect of a fertilizer on plant growth you would use the fertilizer on growing plants. Your experiment would be controlled if you also had some plants growing nearby on which you did not use the fertilizer. A comparison between the two would show how much of the growth was due to the fertilizer and how much to other factors such as sunlight, rain, original condition of the soil, etc.

Control may also take the form of keeping the conditions under which an experiment is performed as nearly as possible the same as those under which it or a similar experiment was previously performed.

If an experiment is completely controlled the variables are reduced to one. Children frequently suggest controls which allow for some of the extraneous variables but not for all of them.

The ratings of the judges were then tabulated and percentages of agreement were determined. It was found that the arrangement of cards in a single group could not be used because of the disagreement among the judges. A tally was made for each situation card showing the number of judges who had placed it in each of the pink card categories. It was finally left in the category in which the largest number of judges had placed it. Frequently there was a tie and in such cases the card was left in the category to which the investigator had assigned it. This was arbitrary and was justified only by the percentages of agreement of each judge with the majority rating. These percentages are affected by the fact that the individual ratings of each judge were utilized in determining the majority rating.

When each card had been placed in a category in this manner, a list was made of the arrangement. The percentages of agreement between each judge's rating and the majority rating of 74 items were as follows:

Judge	*Agreement*
A	88%
B	77
C	65
D	85
E	80
F	79

The cards containing the pertinent references to books or written materials as a source of information were sent to one judge besides the investigator. These cards were to be placed into categories as follows:

1. Suggestion that a specific book be consulted or the actual consultation of a specific book.
2. Suggestion that a specific type of book be consulted.
3. Suggestion that a book be consulted—neither book nor type mentioned specifically.
4. Book from which information is recalled specifically mentioned.
5. Information recalled from a book but book not specifically named.
6. Evidence of misreading a book.
7. Attitudes concerning the use of books.

Each category was written on a pink card which was sent to the judge with the cards containing the pertinent remarks. The judge was an experienced classroom teacher. She was given the following directions:

This set of cards contains examples of the suggestions or use of written materials as sources of information by third grade children. These examples are written in blue ink. The red ink statements serve to orient the response in its situation. The cards should be classified according to the blue ink statements only.

You are requested to classify the cards by arranging them in piles according to the titles on the pink cards. No further classification within a pile is needed. The pink cards are to be placed at the top of their respective piles and the piles then placed on top of each other. Written materials other than books are to be classified as books.

Please do not consult anyone else in connection with this matter.

The agreement between the investigator and the additional judge was 67 per cent. Such a low figure is attributed by the investigator to the use of poorly defined categories. For example, the judges disagreed as to whether the *Book of Knowledge* should be considered a specific book or a specific type of book when the volume was not mentioned. If the definitions of the categories were made more precise, it seemed to the investigator that a high percentage of agreement could probably be reached. Hence it did not seem necessary to redefine them or to have these cards rated by additional judges.

Results from the Classroom Session Records

The results obtained from the classroom session records have been organized around the questions which the study was designed to investigate, namely:

1. What sources of information do children tend to use or suggest in response to various types of problems and what are their attitudes toward such sources?
2. What is the effect of the teacher as far as can be ascertained in determining children's selection of sources of information and attitudes concerning such sources?
3. What sex differences are evident in the children's suggestions of sources of information?

4. What is the relation between sources of information cited and difficulty of problem?

These questions will be taken up in order.

SOURCES OF INFORMATION SUGGESTED

From the running records taken in the classroom it was found that third grade children use or suggest both empirical and authoritarian sources of information. There is no evidence of a general predominance of one type.

An investigation was made to ascertain the extent to which the remarks in the classrooms were scattered among the children. The results are given separately in Table III for sources of information and attitudes.

TABLE III

Distribution of Suggestions Made During 31½ Hours of Classroom Discussions by 120 Children

	No. of Times Suggested	No. of Different Children Making Suggestion
Source of Information		
Experiment.................................	34	26
Observation.................................	17	13
Books.......................................	68	39
Asking someone.............................	8	7
Attitudes		
Appropriateness of source..................	15	11
Reliability of source.......................	5	4
Desirability of proving, checking, repeating.	6	5
Doubt, uncertainty, caution................	10	6

Nearly all branches of science were represented in the situations studied. Many of these followed one another in rapid succession, however. Consequently some were present only to a small extent.

Responses concerning empirical sources of information tended to occur in situations where apparatus or material was at hand. Those giving evidence of authoritarian sources tended to occur in situations where apparatus or material was not present. (Apparatus is considered to be not present unless attention is called to it by the teacher or it is so placed that the children might readily be reminded of it and regard it as intended for their use. Thus it is possible for a lesson held in a room in which apparatus is stored or in which it is set up as a museum exhibit to be classed as a lesson in which no apparatus was present.) This is partly a result of the fact that problems for which only empirical sources of information are suitable tended to occur in situations in which apparatus was at hand and problems for which only authoritarian sources are suitable tended to occur in situations in which apparatus was not at hand. The findings for the total group of situations are shown in Table IV. The

TABLE IV

*Number of Children Suggesting a Source of Information in Biased and Unbiased Classroom Situations Differing as to the Presence of Apparatus**

Source of Information	Situations with Apparatus	Situations without Apparatus	Total
Experiment........................	20	2	22
Reading...........................	3	7	10
Total............................	23	9	32

* In some of the cases, one of the sources of information was not suitable for the problem in question. These cases are the biased situations.

value of chi-square for the data in this table is significant. In about one half of the instances in which books or experiments were suggested only one of these sources was suitable. It was nearly always the one suggested. When this group of biased instances was removed and the remaining half of the instances examined, it was found that there was still a preponderance of empirical suggestions in situations with apparatus and of authoritarian suggestions in non-apparatus situations. However, the value of chi-square for this group was too small to be significant. Whether an increase in the number of cases (there were only 17 in this unbiased group) would make chi-square significant is uncertain. The data for the unbiased situations are presented in Table V.

The actual problem situations during which the suggestion or use of an empirical source of information was recorded in the

TABLE V

Number of Children Suggesting a Source of Information in Unbiased Classroom Situations* Differing as to the Presence of Apparatus

Source of Information	Situations with Apparatus	Situations without Apparatus	Total
Experiment......................	9	1	10
Reading.........................	3	4	7
Total......................	12	5	17

* Only the situations in which either source of information would be suitable have been used here. x^2 is no longer significant (5 per cent probability of chance occurrence). This may be the result of the reduction in the number of cases.

classrooms were written on separate cards and placed in five categories by selected judges as described above. A *majority classification* of the children's responses was prepared, based upon the majority decisions of the judges; that is, each response was placed in the category in which the majority of the judges (six including the investigator) placed it, or in the category in which the investigator had placed it in the event of a tie. There were 74 of these responses in all.

The five categories are stated below and in parentheses preceding each is the number of responses which were placed in that category in the *majority classification:*

(12) 1. Experiments with some measure of control.

(12) 2. Experiments without the suggestion of a control.

(2) 3. Manipulation of materials for the purpose of facilitating observation.

(27) 4. Observation without manipulation but with or without the use of instruments. Visits for the purpose of observation are included.

(21) 5. Attitudes concerning the use of empirical sources of information.

It can be seen that controlled experiments are relatively rare even among the children in the groups studied who have been accustomed to regular science classes weekly or oftener. Simple observation and visiting are most common among the empirical sources of information suggested.

Some examples of responses placed in each of these categories are given below. The italicized statement is the one classified in every case; the other statements serve to orient the statement classified.

1. *Experiments with Some Measure of Control*

CLASSROOM TEACHER: "Do you think after reading this morning that we have our salamanders in a good place?"

1ST CHILD: "I just thought maybe the salamanders would like the light places and the newt the dark; but the newt would go to the other places because he likes to be with the salamanders."

SCIENCE TEACHER: "You mean his desire for company would overcome his desire for darkness."

2ND CHILD: *"If we want to see whether the newt likes the salamanders or the darkness more, we might take the salamanders out for a while."*

The class had made carbon dioxide the preceding day and had lowered a lighted candle into it, expecting the candle to be extinguished, but much to their surprise it had remained burning. They were not sure whether this was because Ted had lowered it carefully or because all the carbon dioxide in the bottle had escaped.

CLASSROOM TEACHER: "What shall we do to interpret the fact that the candle stays lighted when Ted lowered it carefully, as it did yesterday?"

CHILD: *"Take it up and put it down without care."*

The class had been experimenting with a burning candle which became extinguished under an inverted milk bottle.

CHILD: *"There might be a difference in the effect of different bottles on the flame going out." She now tries it with a big beaker.*

1ST CHILD: Performed an experiment he previously read in a book to show that hot air is lighter than cold air. A paper bag was tied on each end of a meter stick. A lighted candle was held under one bag, thus heating the air in it. In the course of the experiment the candle was changed from one bag to the other.

2ND CHILD: "I don't see why one goes up even if hot air does go in because there is warm air in each of them."

3RD CHILD: *"I have an idea. Put one candle under the other bag and two under the first bag." Tries her suggestion.*

CLASSROOM TEACHER: "Would you use a spoon to measure the amount of vinegar?" (to add to soda in making some carbon dioxide gas).

1ST CHILD: "We might get a little too much if we didn't use a spoon."

2ND CHILD: "We can watch the level through a glass bottle." (He does not see the need of using a spoon.)

1ST CHILD: "Yes, but how would we know how high two spoonfuls will go?"

3RD CHILD: *Suggests that we use a spoon this time and then we shall know next time.*

CLASSROOM TEACHER: "Do you think after reading this morning that we have our salamanders in a good place? How could we experiment to find out if they really want sunlight?"

CHILD: *"Put them in a place where part is light and part is dark. See which side they prefer.*

2. *Experiments without the Suggestion of a Control*

1ST CHILD: "In my opinion in a book I read called "Science Stories," it said that if the sun was on the earth it would burn the earth up."

2ND CHILD: *"If you take a magnifying glass and hold it over paper and burn it with the sun's heat, it shows the sun is hot."*

1ST CHILD: "I just thought of something. That magnifying glass— do you mean it would scorch the paper or start a flame fire?"

2ND CHILD: "Scorch it."

3RD CHILD: "My father tried it. He got a flame."

4TH CHILD: *"When I burned it I got a flame."*

The class was experimenting with a candle burning under inverted bottles.

CHILD: *"I have a theory. Do it very slowly so that it can get used to the place." She tries it.*

CLASSROOM TEACHER: "What is in the air that makes things burn?"

1ST CHILD: "Oxygen."

CLASSROOM TEACHER: "How do you know?"

1ST CHILD: *Describes the extinguishing of a candle by inverting a bottle over it.*

The class was making carbon dioxide.

SCIENCE TEACHER: "How do we know whether it is making enough carbon dioxide?"

CHILD: *"Try it with a candle."*

SCIENCE TEACHER: "What happens when cold and warm water are mixed? Have you ever noticed when in the water whether it is colder at the top or bottom?"

CHILD: *Tells about finding warm water on top with the sun. He then plunged his hand down in and found it cold.*

3. Manipulation of Materials for the Purpose of Facilitating Observation

A child asked, "Are those two openings leading out of the air pump—one for hot air and one for cold air?"

SCIENCE TEACHER: "Let's ask John if he knows anything about the pump."

JOHN: *"This one got cold and this one got hot." He tries the pump while the other children observe. He holds his fingers over it, etc.*

A boy had a handkerchief in the bottom of an inverted tumbler which he lowered into water.

SCIENCE TEACHER: "What keeps his handkerchief dry?"

1ST CHILD: "There was water in the glass."

2ND CHILD: "No, there wasn't."

3RD CHILD: *"O.K., now watch it. It won't stay down."*

4. Observation without Manipulation but with or without the Use of Instruments—Visits for the Purpose of Observation Included

The following question came up in class: "Which is the right place for our plants to be, in here (science room) or in our own room?"

CHILD: *"This isn't a good day to decide."*

SCIENCE TEACHER: "Why?"

CHILD: *"Because the sun isn't out. We can't see which way it goes."*

Someone asked a question about the little white things on the side of the aquarium.

1ST CHILD: "They are snail eggs. I have so many. They come all the time."

SCIENCE TEACHER: "Marjorie is offering us a kind of proof. How can we really find out?"

2ND CHILD: *"We could watch them—to see the snails come out. If you saw anything like snails you could look through a microscope."*

The science teacher led an experiment to separate sulphur and iron with a magnet.

1ST CHILD: Tries it.

2ND CHILD: *"I saw one time that all the sulphur seemed to stick on the outside of the end of the magnet and not the middle."*

A child asked whether human beings could live on the sun.

2ND CHILD: "Scientists believe there are no people on the sun but they can't prove it."

3RD CHILD: Suggests that they will be able to find out by looking at the sun through the new big telescope.

4TH CHILD: *"You can't look at the sun through a telescope. It's too bright."*

5TH CHILD: "Prove it."

4TH CHILD: *Relates his own trials with a small telescope.*

SCIENCE TEACHER: "How can we make this water evaporate?"

1ST CHILD: "Turn on the Bunsen burner."

2ND CHILD: *"I let some stand and it evaporated."*

The classroom teacher asked, "Can waves carry rocks?"

CHILD: *"I saw stones moving under water but the waves weren't carrying them."*

5. *Attitudes Concerning the Use of Empirical Sources of Information*

The science teacher suggested, "I'd like you to repeat the second part of the experiment. Why?"

CHILD: "Because——"

ANOTHER CHILD: "How many times is Joseph going to do this experiment?"

JOSEPH: *"As long as it's necessary."*

SCIENCE TEACHER: "We had the same queen bee in a hive for two years."

CHILD: *"How did you know it was the same?"*

1ST CHILD: "I don't think he'll succeed" (in a proposed experiment).

CLASSROOM TEACHER: "Do you advise him not to try?"

1ST CHILD: *"I advise him to try because he might discover something. That is the way scientists find out things."*

SCIENCE TEACHER: "Last time we did an experiment to test Pat's explanation. Did we get an answer to it, John?"

JOHN: "Yes, Pat's father's theory was correct."
ANOTHER CHILD: *"We couldn't prove it."*

The class had been extinguishing a candle by inverting a bottle over it and they were continuing their experiments in an effort to explain it.

CLASSROOM TEACHER: "Is it better to have someone tell you or find out for yourself?"
2ND CHILD: "How about scientists? They don't just ask someone. They experiment."
3RD CHILD: "I think it is best to find out the quickest way."
2ND CHILD: *"But you aren't the one to find it out your way."*

CLASSROOM TEACHER: "Who can make a statement about oxygen and the experiment we did with oxygen that proves that a candle burns in it?"
1ST CHILD: "So far oxygen is the only gas that makes a candle burn." (The class had made several gases and tested them.)
2ND CHILD: Makes a generalization about oxygen and burning.
1ST CHILD: *"Yes, but we didn't make all the gases."*

In addition to classifying responses, four of the six judges (including the investigator) were asked to examine each card for evidence of the five following components of the empirical method:

1. Design of experiment or technique.
2. Observation—includes observation from personal experience.
3. Theory or interpretation.
4. Repetition or need of checking.
5. Control.

This was done partly to determine some of the phases of the empirical method which the children were using and partly to offset the limitations of the previous classification in which a response could be placed in one category only. The results are presented in Table VI. Only those examples considered acceptable by three of the four judges were included.

The suggested sources of information of an authoritarian nature were written on cards and classified by one judge in addition to the investigator. This classification was in some re-

TABLE VI

*Number of Instances when Some Phase of the Empirical Method
Was Used by Children**

Phase	No. of Instances
Design of experiment or technique	14
Observation—includes observation from personal experience	34
Theory or interpretation	7
Repetition or need of checking	11
Control	5

* The instances came from 74 children's statements. Some statements gave evidence of more than one phase of the empirical method.

spects unsatisfactory, as explained on page 19. Each of the seven categories given below is preceded by the number of responses placed by the investigator in that category. There was a total of 75 responses.

(7) 1. Suggestion that a specific book be consulted, or actual consultation of a specific book.

(2) 2. Suggestion that a specific type of book be consulted.

(7) 3. Suggestion that a book be consulted—neither book nor type of book mentioned specifically.

(22) 4. Book from which information is recalled specifically mentioned.

(25) 5. Information recalled from a book but book not specifically mentioned.

(4) 6. Evidence of misreading a book.

(8) 7. Attitudes concerning the use of books.

It is evident that most suggestions for the use of books as a source of information were connected with the recall of information which the child realized would apply to a certain problem. The books in such cases were remembered or forgotten with about equal frequency. When the first three categories are taken together, it is found that the suggestion that a book be consulted as a method of answering a problem was made nearly every time the occasion was suited to it. Recollection of past reading was mentioned more frequently, probably because the children observed were already well read on the subjects they were discussing in class. This can, perhaps, be taken as an indication that the science topics were well within the ability and interest ranges of the children.

The following examples are taken from the investigator's arrangement of the 75 statements in the seven categories:

1. *Suggestion that a Specific Book Be Consulted, or the Actual Consultation of a Specific Book*

1st CHILD: "What is the atmosphere?"
2nd CHILD: *"Look in the dictionary."*

The science teacher asked a boy who was standing on a tin can and was unable to crush it with his weight, "How much do you weigh?"
CHILD WHO HAS BEEN STANDING ON CAN: "I don't know."
ANOTHER CHILD: *Goes to class weight chart at back of room to find first child's weight.*

2. *Suggestion that a Specific Type of Book Be Consulted*

The classroom teacher asked, "How do they tell the weather so long in advance?"
1st CHILD: "We could look it up in the library."
2nd CHILD: *"Look it up in airplane books."*

CLASSROOM TEACHER: "Now what causes cold blasts (in connection with weather discussion) to change? That's a very important question. Who will be responsible for looking that up?—Now I wonder where you are going to find it?"
CHILD: *"In science books."*

3. *Suggestion That a Book Be Consulted—Neither Book nor Type of Book Mentioned Specifically*

CLASSROOM TEACHER: "May I leave this question with the class? (about position of earth in sky.) This will give you something to think about."
CHILD: *"I'm going to look it up in books, too."*

1st CHILD: (giving a report on the musk ox): "He eats lichens."
2nd CHILD: "What is a lichen?"
CLASSROOM TEACHER: "I wonder how we can find out what a lichen is?"
1st CHILD: *"Look it up."*

4. *Book from Which Information Is Recalled Specifically Mentioned*

1st child: *"Yesterday—we didn't know what confederate means. I have it here."* He reads from a dictionary.

Child: "Dinosaurs had very small brains."
Classroom teacher: "I'd like to ask whether this child's statement is correct."
Child: *"It says so here in the book."*

5. *Information Recalled from a Book but Book not Specifically Mentioned*

1st child: "If world hasn't cooled off how can the north and south poles be so cold?"
2nd child: *"I read that the sun does shine on the poles but it hasn't time to warm them."*

Science teacher: "Why do you suppose the moon's surface hasn't been smoothed off?"
Child: *"I read that the moon's atmosphere doesn't stop meteors. If it started to get smoothed off a meteor might hit it and roughen it."*

6. *Evidence of Misreading a Book*

1st child: "Can people really live on the sun?" (Question continued from discussion at previous science period.)
2nd child: *"I think there's a solid part of the sun. It says so in this book."* After he is contradicted, he goes to the book and announces that he has made a mistake because he skipped a line in reading.

Classroom teacher: "When was Mozart born?"
Child: *"1956."* When she is contradicted she looks in the Book of Knowledge again to prove her point.

7. *Attitudes Concerning the Use of Books*

The children were attempting to explain the behavior of a candle when a bottle is inverted over it. The candle was in a pan of water.
1st child: "I know why it does it."
Science teacher: "Are you sure? Why so sure?"
1st child: "I read it somewhere in a book."
2nd child: *"You can't prove it. The book could make a mistake same as you could."*

SCIENCE TEACHER: "Did you mean he's too heavy to swim?"
(dinosaur)
1ST CHILD: "That's what the book said."
2ND CHILD: *"That isn't true, though."*

INFLUENCE OF THE TEACHER IN DETERMINING SOURCES

In general, it is difficult to measure the effect of the teacher in influencing children's use and mention of sources of information and attitudes. This study, however, furnished some evidence that frequent expression of attitudes by the teacher may result in the more frequent expression of similar attitudes by the children in her class. In Table VII it can be seen that Class C, which is represented by more than twice as many expressions of attitudes on the part of the children as other classes, is also the class which is represented by more than twice the number of attitudes expressed by teachers.

TABLE VII

Number of Attitudes Expressed by Children and Teachers* During Several Class Sessions

	Number of Attitude Expressions:	
Class	By Children	By Classroom and Science Teachers
A	0	7
B	11	13
C	28	27
D	2	3
E	9	4
Total	50	54

* The attitude expressions considered are those statements which give evidence of attitudes concerning the appropriateness or reliability of a source of information or the desirability of proving, checking, or repeating experiments; and general statements indicating doubt, uncertainty, or caution.

It was stated on page 7 that the investigator's running records from classrooms were not completely reliable quantitatively because all remarks made in the classroom were not recorded.

Hence the evidence given in Table VII may not be reliable and must be treated merely as an indication of a problem on which further study would be valuable.

In connection with this question some contributary evidence from the interviews is presented on pages 57-59.

SEX DIFFERENCES

All the sources of information suggested in the classroom were mentioned by both boys and girls. From Table VIII it can be seen that 61 per cent of the remarks concerning sources of information were made by boys and that the boys also made con-

TABLE VIII

Distribution of Remarks Made by 120 Boys and Girls in the Classroom

Classified Remark	Boys	Girls	Total	Numerical Total of Remarks
Mention of sources of information.....	61%*	39%	100%	83
All other remarks..................	72	28	100	440

* In this and subsequent tables percentages are expressed to nearest whole number.

siderably more of the extraneous remarks than the girls. In fact, it is possible that the boys suggested more sources of information simply because they spoke oftener than the girls. It is impossible to conclude from this study whether girls suggest sources of information less frequently than boys because they have fewer such ideas or because they are more hesitant about speaking in the classroom.

Although the investigator's running records from classrooms are not altogether reliable the investigator can think of no factors which would contribute to the presence of a sex bias in the records.

The girls suggested 69 per cent of the experiments although the boys mentioned the majority of all the other sources of information (Table IX). In Table X experiment and observation

TABLE IX

Relative Frequencies of Sources of Information Suggested by 120 Boys and Girls in the Classroom

Source of Information	Remarks Made by:			Numerical Total
	Boys	Girls	Total	
Experiment......................	31%	69%	100%	16
Observation...................	56	44	100	16
Reading.........................	74	26	100	43
Asking someone...................	62	38	100	8

are included under *empirical* sources, and reading and asking someone are grouped as authoritarian sources. The girls spoke in the classroom less often than the boys but when they did, they suggested empirical sources as often as authoritarian. The boys, on the other hand, suggested authoritarian sources oftener than empirical. The evidence for this seems to be highly significant statistically, but the data are subject to the many variables present in a classroom situation. Contradictory evidence was found from the interviews. This evidence is discussed somewhat at length later in the study.

TABLE X

*Relative Frequency of Empirical and Authoritarian Sources of Information Mentioned by 120 Boys and Girls in the Classroom**

Source of Information	Boys' Remarks		Girls' Remarks	
	No.	%	No.	%
Empirical......................	14	4	18	12
Authoritarian...................	37	10	14	9
Other remarks.................	316	86	124	79
Total......................	367		156	

* Experiment and observation have been grouped as *empirical* sources, and reading and asking someone are included under *authoritarian*. χ^2 is approximately 9.4, which is highly significant (probability of chance occurrence less than 1 per cent).

EFFECT OF DIFFICULTY OF PROBLEM

The classroom session records gave no information that was applicable to this question. It will be discussed in connection with the interviews in the next chapter.

SUBJECT-MATTER INTERVIEWS

In connection with the classroom session records, it was thought desirable to determine to some extent the amount of subject matter which selected children retained for a period of six weeks after that subject matter had been discussed in class. This was done to determine whether children were getting a lesson worth-while from the point of view of subject matter at the same time that they were getting practice in the use of sources of information. Actually subject matter cannot be entirely separated from methods, but it is possible to throw emphasis on one or the other. The teachers in these classes were trying to emphasize methods. The subject-matter interviews also served as an index as to whether these lessons were well taught, on the assumption that a well-taught lesson would result in some retention of subject matter after a period of six weeks.

For this purpose, two of the third grades from School Y were selected. Each of these consisted of children of similar age and intelligence. The I.Q. and socio-economic levels were rather high. Four boys and four girls were selected from each class as a sample. An attempt was made to choose some children of higher I.Q. and some of lower I.Q. in each sample and for each sex. Some of these children who were selected had contributed to the class discussion and some had not. All had been present on the days of the lessons about which they were questioned.

The children in each sample were interviewed twice. One interview dealt with a class discussion concerning the difference between stars and planets and another dealt with a lesson during which apparatus had been used. The lessons during which apparatus was used were not the same in one class as in the other and were not particularly well matched. It was impossible to find a corresponding lesson of this type in the classes during the time they were studied. A running record of the class discussions about which the interviews were arranged was available. The eight children from a class were all questioned the same morning with the exception of a few absentees. They were all asked not to say anything about the interview to the others in their class.

The discussions concerning stars and planets in each class were similar. The compositions, motions, distances, and directions of each were considered in both classes. Each class discussed some material not taken up by the other, but only the common material was included in the interviews. In each class there was a short demonstration in which children represented stars or planets and stood in various places in the room to indicate the relationships between their distances and directions.

One class had been discussing the water cycle in connection with a study of the atmosphere. They went to the laboratory to find out how to make water evaporate and to observe any phenomena connected with it. They had witnessed a movie on the water cycle in the atmosphere a few days before.

The other lesson in which apparatus was used had resulted from a previous lesson during which a bottle of carbon dioxide had been made. When lowering a lighted candle into this bottle, the children had at first discovered that it became extinguished. Later, however, it was lowered and the flame did not go out. It happened that the boy who lowered it the second time did so with unusual care. Consequently the children were not sure whether the candle had remained burning because the supply of carbon dioxide was exhausted or because of the care used in lowering the candle. They decided to repeat the experiment with a bottle of fresh carbon dioxide and have the same boy lower it with equal care. The class finally concluded that it was because of the exhaustion (as they expressed it) of the carbon dioxide.

These particular lessons were chosen because they were matched in such a way that a set of five questions could be found which would be suitable for children from either class.

Each interview was opened by helping the child recall the lesson in question and asking him to state everything he remembered from it. This was followed by various questions which had not already been answered. In the case of the lesson involving apparatus, the child was asked to state:

1. The purpose of doing the experiment.
2. The technique involved.
3. The theories proposed.
4. The observations.
5. The results.

The questioning concerning the classroom discussions about stars and planets consisted in asking the child to differentiate between stars and planets with respect to:

1. Composition.
2. Motions.
3. Distances from the earth.
4. Directions from the earth.
5. Whether the sun is a star or a planet.

These questions were chosen because they covered the facts which had been emphasized during the class discussions.

The answers given by the children during the interviews designed to test their recollection of subject matter after six weeks were studied by the investigator. Eight of the sixteen children answered satisfactorily four out of five of the questions concerning the lessons in which apparatus was used. Seven children answered four out of five of the questions about the stars and planets in a satisfactory way. The investigator compared the answers of each child during these interviews with the record of that child's contributions during the class discussions, but found no convincing relationships. The number of children questioned was actually too small for this type of evidence to be conclusive.

In examining the children's answers concerning the lesson during which water was evaporated, the investigator found that most of the eight children had a rather inadequate idea of what the lesson had been about. Some of them remembered it only vaguely and one boy decided he must have been absent, though he had been one of the contributors at the time. Several of the children mentioned the movie of the water cycle and knew that the movie had some connection with the lesson in the laboratory, but could not remember what either the movie or the lesson had been about. One girl in the class was an exception in that she understood and recalled the lesson to the investigator's complete satisfaction. This girl had an I.Q. of 152, which was almost the highest in the group, and yet other children with only slightly lower I.Q.'s failed to remember the lesson well at all.

Four of the eight children remembered the purpose of the experiment vaguely. Only one girl remembered it well. Six children remembered the technique used. No one remembered the theories that had been proposed, but these had not been emphasized during the lesson. Four children were able to discuss the observations slightly and one other girl remembered them well. This same girl also remembered the results. Two other children knew something of the results.

The other group of children were questioned about the lesson during which they examined the effect of carbon dioxide on a candle flame. Six of these children remembered the lesson to the investigator's satisfaction. Their greatest difficulty was in trying to recall the theories or hypotheses that they had shown to be erroneous. Most of them remembered the hypothesis that had been correct and the way in which it had been demonstrated.

Six of the eight children recalled something about the purpose of the experiment. Three of these remembered it well. Four children remembered the technique well and a fifth remembered it less satisfactorily. All eight of the children remembered something about the theory that was accepted, although two were vague. They all remembered that other theories had been disproved but they did not know what these other theories had been. Three children discussed the observations well and three others were able to say something in answer to this question. Four children remembered the results.

The investigator noted that the conclusions of the children during the interview were worded in just as specific and particular a manner as had been done in the classroom at the time of the lesson. For example; no child said that the carbon dioxide would extinguish a candle flame although that is what they had proved. Instead, they tended to say that "The candle could burn if the carbon dioxide was a little bit exhausted"; or "We proved that the candle went out because the carbon dioxide had escaped"; or "We discovered that it was because the carbon dioxide was exhausted." No attempt was made in the classroom to get the children to word their conclusion in more general terms. Such an attempt might have had results that would have been evident six weeks later. None of the children remembered which chemicals had been mixed to make the carbon dioxide, but this was incidental to the real problem.

In comparing the two classes in which the interview results were so different, the investigator thinks that the explanation lies in a more effective technique used by the second classroom teacher. She managed the group well at all times and was able to interest them to do their best thinking. In the group which was studying the water cycle, the children were not uninterested and yet they did not seem to be giving quite their fullest attention. When the investigator spoke to the teacher who had worked with carbon dioxide, she claimed that she usually did not have so much success with her classes but explained her achievement this year on the basis of the group she was fortunate enough to have. She was especially interested in the experimental procedure as a method of solving problems and wished to interest the children in it.

The two classes which differed in the extent of remembering their lessons with apparatus were more similar in their recall of the facts they had learned about stars and planets. The children in the interviews were first asked to tell all the differences they knew between stars and planets. Every child could give some information before he was questioned further. Only half of the eight children from each class gave four out of the five items even when questioned specifically on each item, but every child except one answered at least two questions and there was no child who was not sure of some of his information. The investigator considered that the children had retained enough to have made the lessons worth while. The children seemed to have most difficulty with the question concerning the difference between stars and planets with respect to motions. This is probably because this question tends to be farther removed from the children's interests than the others that were asked. The investigator has frequently heard children both inside and outside classes ask what the stars are made of, but has seldom heard them ask whether the stars move.

Eleven of the sixteen children knew something about what the stars are made of. One of those was vague, however. Eight children answered the question about motions, but three of these were vague. Twelve children knew about the relative distances of stars from the earth as compared with planets. Thirteen children knew that the sun is a star. Thirteen also remembered something about the directions of the stars from the earth.

The running records of the four class discussions which were involved were sent to two classroom teachers who were asked to read them and answer the following questions about each one:

1. Which children do you think really got something out of the class? Underline their names.
2. Do you think the lesson was justified from the point of view of the proportion of the children who responded?
3. Would you still say that the lesson was valuable to the children whose names you have underlined if they did not remember much of it after a period of six weeks?
4. Do you think the lesson was valuable to the children who did not respond?
5. Would your answer to number 4 depend on whether these children remembered much of the lesson after six weeks?

One of the classroom teachers was the teacher of one of the two classes in which the children were interviewed and the other was a critic teacher who had never seen the children. The investigator used the responses of these teachers to modify her interpretations of the subject-matter interviews from the point of view of the justifiability of those interpretations. Neither teacher made a definite statement as to which lessons were good or inferior or which children did or did not benefit from the lessons. These teachers did, however, mention some relative values which were in agreement with the investigator's conclusions.

In summary, the investigator considered all the lessons involved in this part of the study to have been worth while, with the exception of the lesson connected with a study of the water cycle. The following reasons may account for some of the difficulty with this lesson:

1. The teacher failed to gain completely the children's interest.
2. The experiment was forced upon the children too suddenly. Even at the time some children were probably uncertain why the experiment was being performed.
3. The movie concerning the water cycle was too difficult for the children. It would have been clearer if it had been repeated after the experiment.
4. The teacher did not clinch the lesson by a "Follow up," such as repetition, discussion, or further experiment.

The investigator does not wish to imply that a study of the water cycle in the atmosphere is too difficult for the third grade, but merely that it requires more time than was allotted to it in this instance. It is difficult to evaluate a class, however, unless the ultimate goals are known. At times such goals may give value to a lesson which seems unsatisfactory when judged by itself. The reader should, therefore, take this analysis with caution.

CHAPTER III

Individual Interviews

Two types of questions were made the basis for two sets of interviews. One set of interviews was made up of questions of the "How would you find out?" type. A second set was composed of questions of the "How did you find out?" type. Each set will be discussed separately.

"How Would You Find Out?" Interviews

Six questions starting with the words, "How would you find out?" and six starting, "How would you prove?" were divided into two sets and asked during separate interviews with each child. A few other questions were interspersed with them. These were originally designed for a branch of the study which had later to be discarded because of insufficient time to investigate the matter adequately and because it did not bear upon the main subject of study. The actual arrangement follows:

First Interview

1. How would you find out whether snow is as cold as ice?
2. Why does sugar dissolve faster in hot water than in cold?
3. How would you prove that string bean plants will not grow without water?
4. How do you know that the earth is round?
5. How would you prove that woolen clothes keep you warmer than cotton clothes?
6. How would you find out how many fins there are on a fish?
7. How do you know that water will put out a fire?
8. Why do you have to squeeze a sponge before you can make it sink?

Second Interview

1. How would you prove that some of your friends are heavier than you are?

41

2. How would you find out what a bluebird builds his nest out of?
3. How would you find out how cold snow is?
4. How would you prove whether snow is as cold as ice?
5. Why do we have snow only in cold weather?
6. How would you prove whether a cat will be thin unless he has some food besides fish to eat?
7. How would you find out when there will be another full moon?
8. Why does daylight last longer on a summer day than it does on a winter day?
9. How would you find out where the part of an automobile called the distributor is located?
10. How would you prove that the earth goes around the sun?

The foregoing indicates the order in which questions were asked of the children. The questions which were finally used in the analysis are given below in the order of increasing difficulty. The criterion of difficulty was taken as the number of "I don't know" answers. Failure to answer a question at all was interpreted as an "I don't know" answer. The numbers in the parentheses before the number of each question indicate the percentage of "I don't know" answers out of the total for that question. One hundred and forty-four children were interviewed, but some children said, "I don't know" first, and later gave a different answer, and some gave an answer first and later said, "I don't know." In cases in which two answers were given to a single question the responses were treated as separate answers. Rarely did a child give three answers to a question, but in such cases all three were discarded.

The "How would you find out?" questions are listed separately from the "How would you prove?" questions.

(3%) 1. How would you find out what a bluebird builds his nest out of?
(6%) 2. How would you find out how many fins there are on a fish?
(12%) 3. How would you find out how cold snow is?
(15%) 4. How would you find out where the part of an automobile called the distributor is located?
(18%) 5. How would you find out when there will be another full moon?
(21%) 6. How would you find out whether snow is as cold as ice?

(4%) 7. How would you prove that some of your friends are heavier than you are?

(12%) 8. How would you prove whether snow is as cold as ice?

(18%) 9. How would you prove that woolen clothes keep you warmer than cotton clothes?

(22%) 10. How would you prove whether a cat will be thin unless he has some food besides fish to eat?

(23%) 11. How would you prove that string bean plants will not grow without water?

(45%) 12. How would you prove that the earth goes around the sun?

All the children in each of the five third grade classes that were observed were interviewed. In addition, six boys and six girls from each of two first, third, and fifth grades (72 in all) were interviewed. These children were selected randomly from classes in a large city public school where there were no regular classes in science in these grades. They were added for the purpose of testing whether there is any change in the sources of information which children suggest as they become older. This and one other part of the study freed it from the confines of the third grade. The 24 children from the two third grades of this large city public school were included with the 120 children from Schools X and Y previously mentioned to make up the 144 children whose responses were used to determine the percentages given above in connection with the interview questions.

Both sets of questions were answered by the same group of children.

Each interview was given to all the children in a class in as short a space of time as possible in order to minimize the opportunity for talking about the questions before all had been interviewed. Each child was requested not to say anything about the questions to the children who had not yet been interviewed. In some cases, the interviews with members of a given class were nearly completed in one morning or in one day. In others, a period of a week or more elapsed before all the children of the same class were interviewed.

The questions were repeated as often as necessary and were slightly reworded for some of the first grade children. If the child gave an unsatisfactory answer the question was repeated, or he was asked some further question such as: "Do you think that would prove it?", "Is that what you would do to find out?", or "How would *you* do it?" If, after repeating a question, a child gave no answer at all, it was assumed that his answer was the same as "I don't know."

"How Did You Find Out?" Interviews

In the "How did you find out?" interview, each child was asked eight questions. These questions were so chosen that it was expected most of the children could answer them. Following the child's answer to each question he was asked, "How did you find that out?" It was the answer to this question in every case which was of interest in this study.

The subjects for this interview were 15 boys and 15 girls from second grade classes, 10 boys and 10 girls from fourth grades, and 10 boys and 10 girls from sixth grades. Thus there was a total of 70 children. They were taken from a small city public school and were of comparatively low I.Q. and socio-economic status.

The eight questions were as follows:

1. Are the stars always in the same place every night?
2. What time of year do people plant seeds in the gardens?
3. Does the sun always set at the same time every day?
4. Are there more thunderstorms in the summer or the winter?
5. Do birds which stay here in the winter have baby birds in the winter?
6. Do birds eat anything besides worms?
7. Do leaves fall off trees mostly in the summer, fall, winter, or spring?
8. When does Easter come?

Whereas the previous interviews were directed at the future, the "How did you find out?" questions dealt with opinions or conclusions that already had been formulated. Of course, it is recognized that the children probably did not remember the actual sources of their information but it is assumed that the sources named were those which seemed to them appropriate for the information under consideration and which they had probably used at one time or other.

Treatment of Data from Interviews

The answers given by the children during the interview in which they were asked "How would you find out?" and "How would you prove?" questions (pages 42 and 43) were classified under six headings as follows:

1. No answer or "I don't know."
2. Suggestion of observation or experiment.
3. Suggestion involving reading.
4. Suggestion involving asking some other person.
5. Some attempt at reasoning.
6. Miscellaneous.

It is impossible to separate reasoning entirely from the use of a source of information as it is involved frequently in the appraisal of the source and in the selection of those facts most pertinent to the problem. It was the intent of the present questions to have the child indicate a source of information for the fact mentioned in each question. Some children, however, attempted to derive this fact from related facts without mentioning any source. In such cases each child's answer was classified as an attempt at reasoning, because, in a sense, he was using this reasoning to replace a direct source of information.

Twenty children's papers were classified by a second examiner. These papers were chosen so that there was one of a girl and one of a boy from each class with the exception of one first grade in which the I.Q.'s were low. In all there were 240 questions on these twenty papers. The second examiner and the investigator agreed in the classification of 85 per cent of the 240 questions. The 15 per cent of the 240 questions in which there was disagreement between the investigator and the second examiner were distributed among the answer groups as shown in Table XI.

TABLE XI

Disagreement of Check Classification of 240 Questions Made by Second Examiner

Investigator's Classification	Percentage Disagreement
1. No answer or "I don't know"..............................	4%
2. Suggestion of observation or experiment.....................	5
3. Suggestion involving reading..............................	1
4. Suggestion involving asking some other person..............	1
5. Some attempt at reasoning...............................	2
6. Miscellaneous...	2
Total percentage disagreement............................	15%

A few examples of children's answers are included here to show the investigator's analysis which is given in parenthesis following the answer. These samples are all taken from third grade children.

QUESTION 1. How would you find out what a bluebird builds his nest out of?

ANSWERS: "Watch him." (observation)

"You could watch one and see where he goes and how he builds it, I think." (observation)

"It shows in books and you could see it if you could get a bluebird's nest. The books are better because you could see it more clearly." (reading)

QUESTION 2. How would you find out how many fins there are on a fish?

ANSWERS: "Count them." (observation or experiment)

"By catching a fish and counting them. Maybe a magnifying glass would let you see them better." (observation or experiment)

"Read in a book or catch a fish and count them. The book is better because the fish may have some fins that are hard to see." (reading)

QUESTION 3. How would you find out how cold snow is?

ANSWERS: "I could touch it or look it up in a book." (observation or experiment and reading)

"Snow freezes into ice. This proves that snow is as cold as ice if it freezes into ice." (attempt at reasoning)

"By putting a thermometer into it." (observation or experiment)

QUESTION 4. How would you find out where the part of an automobile called the distributor is located?

ANSWERS: "I'd ask my father." (asking someone)

"Look it up in automobile books." (reading)

"I'd ask a mechanic. They ought to know." (asking someone)

QUESTION 5. How would you find out when there will be another full moon?

ANSWERS: "Watch the moon." (observation)

"Look at the calendar." (reading)

"Stay outside until you see another full moon come." (observation)

QUESTION 6. How would you find out whether snow is as cold as ice?

ANSWERS: "Put a thermometer in it. Stick it in the snow and leave it for a while—about 15 minutes—then take it out. That would tell you whether snow is as cold as ice." (experiment or observation)

"I'd look it up in a book. If I couldn't find it in the book, I'd go to some others." (reading)

"Put snow on one part of table and ice on other. Put finger on each at once. But I couldn't be positive at all because my hand might be different from the temperature of the snow or ice." (observation or experiment)

QUESTION 7. How would you prove that some of your friends are heavier than you are?

ANSWERS: "By going and weighing them in a drug store." (observation or experiment)

"I'd weigh myself and them too." (observation or experiment)

"Have them sit on me in the car." (observation or experiment)

QUESTION 8. How would you prove whether snow is as cold as ice?

ANSWERS: "Put a thermometer on snow and one on ice. See if both stay the same." (observation or experiment)

"I would look it up in a lot of books. You can't prove it." (reading)

"Snow freezes into ice." (attempt at reasoning)

QUESTION 9. How would you prove that woolen clothes keep you warmer than cotton clothes?

ANSWERS: "If I had any I'd put on a woolen glove on one hand and a cotton glove on the other, but it would still be like the first question, I wouldn't be sure." (observation or experiment)

"Wool clothes are thicker than cotton clothes and maintain heat more." (attempt at reasoning)

"Try it out. Put on thin clothes on a very cold day." (observation or experiment)

QUESTION 10. How would you prove whether a cat will be thin unless he has some food besides fish to eat?
ANSWERS: "Watch him eat fish every day. See if he gets smaller or fatter." (observation or experiment)

"Try it. Give him something besides fish. Weigh him and see whether he got fat or not." (observation or experiment)

"I'd have two cats and give one fish and the other foods." (experiment or observation)

QUESTION 11. How would you prove that string beans will not grow without water?
ANSWERS: "I could look that up in books, too, to prove it." (reading)

"Plant them and not put water on them." (observation or experiment)

"I should think you would have to go out and watch them all the time." (observation or experiment)

QUESTION 12. How would you prove that the earth goes around the sun?
ANSWERS: "Ask the science teacher." (asking someone)

"Because different parts of the earth have seasons at different times. Some have summer while others have winter." (attempt at reasoning)

"Look it up in books. Scientists have found it out." (reading)

The classified scores were tabulated and examined by the chi-square technique to determine whether there were any sex, I.Q., school, and class relationships. The relative predominance of the various types of answers was studied. The questions were arranged in order of difficulty, using as a criterion the percentage of answers which indicated that the child did not know. The product-moment coefficient of correlation was used to determine the relationship between type of suggestion (empirical or authoritarian) given in answer and difficulty of question. The type of suggestion was expressed as the percentage of answers which indicated an empirical suggestion out of all those which indicated either an empirical or an authoritarian suggestion; the children failing to answer the question and those who gave miscellaneous answers were disregarded before the percentage was taken. (There were 10 miscellaneous answers out of a possible 1,728.) The difficulty of the question was, of course, expressed as the percentage of answers which indicated that the child did not know.[1]

The interviews during which children were asked questions and then asked, "How did you find that out?" were analyzed and classified in the same categories as above. The author's classification was not checked by a second examiner because of the similarity of the process with the classification of the other interviews. The preponderance of types of suggestions given in answers was noted. The chi-square technique was used to determine whether there were any significant differences between boys and girls.

RESULTS OBTAINED FROM THE INTERVIEWS

In making up Tables XII, XIII, XV, and XVI, the number of answers has been tabulated rather than the number of children. If a child gave two answers to a single question, each answer was treated separately. When asked, "How would you prove

[1] Actually there were two sampling errors in this study—an error due to the sampling of questions, and an error due to the sampling of children. Two different percentages of children have been reported: namely, the percentage indicating an empirical suggestion, and the percentage unable to answer. The correlation considered is a correlation between these two percentages for each question in the list. Therefore, a test of significance of the correlation coefficient relates to the generalization from these questions to a population of questions of which these may be considered a random sample. Sampling errors in the population of children would have the effect of attaching random errors of measurement to the percentages, and such errors would tend to attenuate the value of the correlation. The magnitude of the effect of a sampling error for the population of children has not been estimated.

TABLE XII

Number and Per Cent of Instances of Sources of Information Suggested by 144 Children in Answer to the "How Would You Find Out?" Questions*

Question	Experiment or Observation		Reading or Using Charts		Asking Someone		Attempt at Reasoning		Total	
	No.	%	No.	%	No.	%	No.	%	No.	%
What bird builds nest of.........	122	84%	18	12%	5	3%			145	99%
How many fins on fish............	127	91	12	9	1	1			140	101
How cold snow is..	126	97	3	2	1	1			130	100
Where automobile distributor is...	55	36	19	12	79	52			153	100
When there is a full moon..........	37	31	63	53	10	8	8	7%	118	99
Whether snow is as cold as ice......	94	85	15	14	2	2			111	101
Total..........	561	69	130	16	98	12	8	1	797	98

* The "I don't know" answers were deducted from the totals before calculating the percentages.

that string bean plants will not grow without water?" one girl replied, "Because the water has to give food to the roots." The investigator asked further, "Does that prove that string beans will not grow without water?" and the girl answered, "Test it. Grow one and don't put any water on it and leave it." Her first answer was analyzed as an attempt at reasoning and her second as an experiment. Each answer was treated as a separate tally in the tabulation.

Hence the number of answers for a question is sometimes greater than the number of children. In rare instances (12 cases out of a possible 1,728) when a child gave three answers to a single question, all three were discarded. This was justified on the assumption that the child had perhaps misunderstood the intent of the question and thought he was expected to give all possible sources of information, or that he was so uncertain of the way he would find his information that his answer was not valuable. Occasionally a child mentioned two items that would fall under the same category, such as describing two possible experiments. In these cases only one tally was made.

The results from the interviews will be organized around the questions which the study was designed to investigate, namely:

1. What sources of information do children tend to use or suggest in response to various types of problems and what are their attitudes toward such sources?
2. What is the effect of the teacher (as far as can be ascertained) in determining children's selection of sources of information and attitudes concerning such sources?
3. What sex differences are evident in the children's suggestions of sources of information?
4. What is the relation between sources of information cited and difficulty of problem?

These questions will be discussed in order in the following pages.

Sources of Information Suggested

Although authoritarian methods were suggested by children in the classroom just as frequently as empirical methods, there was a decided predominance of empirical suggestions in all the interviews. It can be seen from Tables XII and XIII that *experiment* or *observation* constituted 69 per cent and 74 per cent of all the suggestions made by the 144 third grade children on the six "How find out?" and the six "How prove it?" questions respectively. Data in Table XIV show similar results with the first, third, and fifth grade children who were interviewed. These came from the city school in which there was no regular science instruction. Of all the suggestions they made for the six "How find out?" and the six "How prove it?" questions together, 67 per cent to 71 per cent were *experiment* or *observation*. The eight "How did you find out?" questions are treated in Table XV. Here, too, for grades two, four, and six, the *experi-*

TABLE XIII

*Number and Per Cent of Instances of Sources of Information Suggested by 144
Children in Answer to the "How Would You Prove?" Questions**

Question	Experiment or Observation		Reading or Using Charts		Asking Someone		Attempt at Reasoning		Total	
	No.	%	No.	%	No.	%	No.	%	No.	%
Some friends are heavier than you	129	98%			2	2%			131	100%
Whether snow is as cold as ice	109	87	3	2	1	1	12	10	125	100
That woolen clothes keep you warmer	69	56	2	2			53	43	124	101
Whether cat needs food besides fish	101	86	3	3	2	2	12	10	118	101
That plants will not grow without water	85	69	5	4	1	1	32	26	123	100
That earth goes around sun	14	22	16	25	9	14	26	40	65	101
Total	507	74	29	4	15	2	135	20	686	100

* The "I don't know" answers were deducted from the total before calculating
the percentages.

TABLE XIV

*Relative Frequency of Suggestion of Various Sources of Information
in Different Grades**

Source of Information	Grades		
	1	3	5
Experiment or observation	71%	67%	71%
Reading	5	6	9
Asking someone	12	8	9
Attempt at reasoning	12	20	12
Total	100	101	101

* Percentages were calculated after the "I don't know" answers had been
deducted. Each of the three grades was represented by 24 children. There were
72 children in all. Each child was asked 12 questions.

ment or *observation* suggestions make up from 68 per cent to 74 per cent of all the suggestions.

Of course, this relationship does not hold for individual questions. Taking the first question in Table XV, "Are the stars always in the same place every night?" it may be seen that the percentage of empirical suggestions dropped between the second grade and the sixth. On the other hand, the percentage of reading on this subject increased remarkably between these two grades, as would be expected. There seems to be a temporary increase in empirical suggestions for this question in the fourth grade. This can perhaps be explained by the fact that fourth grade children seem to have nearly passed the stage where they take someone's word for something, but have not yet reached the stage where they read much about the stars. The increased opportunity for the fourth grade children to be out-of-doors after dark is also a factor.

In answer to the question, "Are there more thunderstorms in summer or in winter?", there is an increase in the percentage of children making empirical suggestions from grade two to grade four and again to grade six. Here a fact which is true of most of the "How did you find out?" questions may be noted, namely, that the older children tend to avoid using someone else's word as a reason for their beliefs.

Going back to the twelve questions used in compiling Table XIV it is apparent that the suggestion of asking someone for information is made a little more frequently in grade one than in grades three and five. Here, also, reading is suggested slightly more often in the higher grades.

In both Tables XIV and XV the number of children included is too small to accept the results as anything but suggestive.

In Tables XII and XIII, however, the figures presented are considerably more significant. There is decided variation between individual questions in these tables, but for the majority of questions empirical suggestions are prominent. In the question, "How would you find out where the part of an automobile called the distributor is located?", the suggestion of *asking someone* was made by more children than that of *observation*.

TABLE XV

Per Cent of Instances of Sources of Information Suggested by Children in Answer to "How Did You Find Out?" Questions*

Question	GRADE 2					GRADE 4					GRADE 6				
	Experiment or Observation	Reading	Asking Someone	Attempt at Reasoning	Total	Experiment or Observation	Reading	Asking Someone	Attempt at Reasoning	Total	Experiment or Observation	Reading	Asking Someone	Attempt at Reasoning	Total
Are stars in same place every night?	76%	0%	24%	0%	100%	87%	6%	0%	6%	99%	56%	39%	6%	0%	101%
What time of year plant seeds in garden?	80	0	17	3	100	67	5	19	10	101	60	15	10	15	100
Does sun set same time every day?	69	12	19	0	100	85	0	15	0	100	69	15	15	0	99
More thunderstorms in summer or winter?	64	0	23	14	101	89	6	6	0	101	95	0	0	5	100
Do birds have baby birds in winter?	72	11	6	11	100	33	13	0	53	99	40	0	0	60	100
Do birds eat besides worms?	87	7	0	7	101	94	0	6	0	100	100	0	0	0	100
Do leaves fall off mostly in summer, fall, etc.?	93	3	3	0	99	79	11	5	5	100	100	0	0	0	100
When does Easter come?	15	0	69	15	99	0	36	64	0	100	0	81	19	0	100
	74	4	16	5	99	69	9	13	9	100	68	18	6	7	99

* Percentages were calculated after the "I don't know" answers had been deducted from the total. There were 30 children from the second grade, 20 from the fourth grade, and 20 from the sixth grade.

This is what would be expected in view of the fact that few, if any, third grade children know what a distributor is or what it resembles. The investigator questioned a few of the children who suggested *observation* and was told that they had indicated the method they would use *if* they knew what the distributor looked like. The question is probably far above the third grade level of suitability. and was answered by some children on the assumption that they had a background equivalent to that of older people for whom the question would be suitable. There is no pronounced sex difference in this tendency to assume an older background.

In response to the question, "How would you find out when there will be another full moon?", over half the suggestions were connected with the use of the calendar. In this case that is the most suitable source of information for these children and it is readily accessible as well. This question revealed their misunderstanding of the behavior of the moon as, for example, the boy who said he would go outside at night and wait for it.

Children answered the "How would you prove it?" questions in general as if they had been worded, "How would you find out?" The investigator suspected this and questioned several of the children about the meaning of the word *prove*. Most of the children questioned thought that it meant *to find out*. Hence the "How would you prove it?" questions must be analyzed without reference to the word *prove*.

In response to some of these questions the percentage of empirical suggestions was unusually low. When children were asked, "How would you prove that woolen clothes keep you warmer than cotton clothes?", many of them attempted a kind of reasoning. The reasoning was inadequate as a rule. It had to do with such ideas as the wool keeps sheep warm and so it must be warm, or simply that wool is warm because it comes from sheep. Some children who used this type of argument did not know where cotton comes from.

The question with the lowest percentage of empirical suggestions (22 per cent) was, "How would you prove that the earth goes around the sun?" Forty per cent of the answers were attempts at some kind of reasoning but none of these was entirely satisfactory. Some children showed confusion concerning the revolution of the earth around the sun and its rotation on its axis. The 22 per cent of empirical suggestions made were also unsatisfactory. The question was obviously beyond the ability level of most of these children, although many of the children who suggested *asking someone* or *reading* were giving a suitable answer.

The question, "How would you prove that some of your friends are heavier than you are?", which was easiest for the children, brought forth almost entirely empirical suggestions. In fact, it appears that the children may tend to suggest empirical sources of information less frequently as the question becomes more and more difficult for them. This is discussed later in the chapter.

There were three questions in which a substantial percentage (26%–43%) of answers were attempts to reason. These were, "How would you prove that woolen clothes keep you warmer than cotton clothes?", "How would you prove that string bean plants will not grow without water?", and "How would you prove that the earth goes around the sun?" In the case of the first two, the children were doubtless familiar with the statements made in the questions and since most of them probably misunderstood the meaning of the word *prove,* they very likely thought they were being asked how they would find out something they already knew. This explains why some children answered these questions at first as though they had been "Why?" questions instead of "How would you prove?" questions. Some of the attempts at reasoning offered in connection with these two questions led the investigator to think that this was not infrequently the case. In the case of the last question, however, "How would you prove that the earth goes around the sun?", this may not be true. Though the fact was probably familiar to most of the children, it was less a part of their everyday experience than woolen clothes and string bean plants and hence there would be less likelihood of interpreting the question as a "Why?" question. The large percentage of *attempts at reasoning* for this question are very likely connected with a vagueness in the minds of the children because the question was above their mental age level.

The question arises as to whether children dealing with questions suited to them would be more influenced by the suitability or by the accessibility of a source. This question is not answered altogether by this study but some evidence is available in the comparison between the sources of information which children mentioned in the classroom and those suggested during the interviews. In the classroom, authoritarian sources were suggested as frequently as empirical sources. The apparent discrepancy between the findings from the classroom records and from the interviews is perhaps explained by the fact that children making suggestions in the classroom do so from practical considerations. They are aware that they may be called upon to carry out their own suggestions. Hence the relative amounts of time involved and the availability of materials become important. During an interview, on the other hand, it is doubtful that many of the children expect to have to act on their suggestions. This does not imply that the children were insincere in their statements, but merely that one's armchair thinking, so to speak, is often carried out on a more elaborate scale than one's activity.

The sources of information suggested in the classroom were largely suitable for the information required but accessibility was evidently a factor. The tendency for empirical sources to be mentioned when apparatus was at hand and for authoritarian sources to be mentioned when there was no apparatus near by has been mentioned. Although this relationship is not by any means proved in this study, it nevertheless is in agreement with the other findings.

INFLUENCE OF THE TEACHER IN DETERMINING SOURCES

With regard to the "How would you find out?" and the "How would you prove?" interviews, there were some interesting class differences. The three classes in School Y were not significantly different; but the two classes in School X differed very

TABLE XVIA

Relative Frequencies of Sources of Information Given in Answer to Twelve Questions by Children from Two Classes of School X*

Class	Experiment and Observation	Reading	Asking Someone	Attempt at Reasoning	Numerical Total
A................	64%	20%	8%	7%	283
D................	77	10	4	9	272
Total...........	71	15	6	8	575

* The twelve questions include the six "How find out?" and the six "How prove it?" questions. If a child gave two answers to a single question, each answer was treated separately. Hence the number of answers is greater than the number of children. See page 49.

TABLE XVIB

Some Data from Table XVIA Expressed as Numerical Frequencies*

Class	Experiment and Observation	Reading	Total
A.....................................	182	57	239
D.....................................	226	28	254
Total................................	408	85	493

* Only children suggesting experiment, observation, or reading have been included. A highly significant value of χ^2 indicates a probable difference between these classes in the tendency to suggest reading or experiment and observation as a source of information. If children who suggested asking someone are grouped with those suggesting reading (both are authoritarian sources of information) then χ^2 becomes even larger. These values of χ^2 were such that the probability of occurrence by chance was less than 2 per cent.

significantly (less than 2 per cent probability of chance occurrence) with respect to frequencies of suggestions of sources of information (see Table XVIB). When only those children who suggested experiment, observation, or reading in answer to a question were included, it was found that there was a tendency for children from Class A to suggest reading more often and experiment and observation less often than children from Class D. Table XVIA gives the percentages of answers which mention the various sources of information.

A study of Table XVII in this connection will reveal that Class A, in which there was an emphasis on reading as a source of information in the interviews, was also the class in which the teacher made all her source remarks in terms of reading; and Class D, in which there was an emphasis on empirical sources (experiment and observation) in the interviews, was one in which the teacher made more mention of empirical sources in the classroom. These interviews were held with each child individually, apart from the teacher and fellow pupils.

TABLE XVII

Total Number of Times Sources of Information Were Mentioned by Classroom and Science Teachers During All Class Sessions that Were Recorded

Class	Sources of Information		
	Experiment	Observation	Reading
A	0	0	7
B	3	3	12
C	6	0	0
D	7	1	1
E	6	1	4

Data in Table XVII also show that the teachers in Class B and Class C mentioned one type of source of information more often than others; and yet these classes did not differ significantly in their results during the interviews. This may possibly be explained by the fact that these classes had the same science teacher present and were conducted somewhat on the same pattern. Class A, however, made little or no use of the science teacher and was conducted quite differently from Class D which utilized regularly the science teacher available in that school.

SEX DIFFERENCES

The sex differences observed in the classroom records were not corroborated by the interviews with the children. The "How would you prove it?", "How would you find out?", and "How did you find out?" interviews all agreed in exhibiting no significant sex differences.

Further study is needed before a satisfactory interpretation of this discrepancy can be made. The sex differences in the classroom may be of a relatively superficial nature and must be treated accordingly.

EFFECT OF DIFFICULTY OF PROBLEM

The effect of the difficulty of a problem on the choice of a source of information was studied in connection with the "How would you find out?" and the "How would you prove it?" interviews. As described on pages 48-49, this was done by means of a product-moment correlation coefficient between the percentage of answers which indicated that the child did not know, and the percentage of answers which indicated an empirical source of information out of all those which indicated either an empirical or an authoritarian source.

The value of the product-moment correlation was roughly —.65 which is significant (5 per cent probability of chance occurrence), but not highly significant. This, of course, refers to only a sample of the population of children. It provides some indication of a decrease in the proportion of suggested sources of information which are empirical with an increase in difficulty of question for the sample of children who were interviewed. The percentage of answers which indicated that a child did not know was taken as the index of difficulty.

The correlation coefficient was calculated from data presented in Table XVIII.

In view of the doubtful significance of the correlation coefficient and of the fact that it may be argued that some of the questions lend themselves more to one type of answer than to another, it must be concluded that the evidence with regard to the relation between sources of information cited and difficulty of problem is not definite but merely serves to set forth a possibility which, in the opinion of the investigator, is worthy of further study.

It can be seen from Table XVIII that questions 6 and 10 were connected with a higher percentage of empirical sources

TABLE XVIII

Relation Between Percentage of Answers which Indicated that the Child Did Not Know and Percentage of Answers which Indicated an Empirical Rather than an Authoritarian Source of Information

"How Find Out?" and "How Prove It?" Questions*	Answers Indicating an Empirical Source	n†	Answers Indicating that Child Did Not Know	n
1......................	84%	145	3%	158
7......................	98	131	4	145
2......................	91	140	6	152
8......................	87	125	12	146
3......................	97	130	12	148
4......................	36	153	15	187
5......................	31	118	18	161
9......................	56	124	18	159
6......................	85	111	21	150
10.....................	86	118	22	160
11.....................	69	123	23	164
12.....................	22	65	45	148

* Questions are numbered as on pages 42–43.
† This column comprises the totals used for the preceding percentage values in the calculation of the coefficient of correlation.

of information than would be expected if the relationship with the difficulty of the question held strictly. Question 6 was, "How would you find out whether snow is as cold as ice?" Question 10 was worded, "How would you prove whether a cat will be thin unless he has some food besides fish to eat?" Both these questions are so worded as to suggest a comparison. Compare, for example, Question 3, "How would you find out how cold snow is?" Here the child is asked for a simple fact. It may be that a comparison suggested in the wording of a question influences a child toward giving an empirical source of information.

There are also two questions which called forth a lower percentage of empirical suggestions than might have been expected.

Question 4, "How would you find out where the part of an automobile called the distributor is located?" and question 5, "How would you find out when there will be another full moon?" called for information which was not so readily accessible to third grade children by an empirical method of inquiry as was the case with some of the other questions.

CHAPTER IV

Summary and Recommendations

A STUDY was made of the sources of information used or expressed by children in connection with problem situations especially in science. Expressions of attitudes toward these sources were also included. The investigation centered about four questions as follows:

1. What sources of information do children tend to use or suggest in response to various types of problems and what are their attitudes toward such sources?
2. What is the effect of the teacher as far as can be ascertained in determining children's selection of sources of information and attitudes concerning such sources?
3. What sex differences are evident in the children's suggestions of sources of information?
4. What is the relation between sources of information cited and difficulty of problem?

Running records of classroom discussion in science from five third grade classes distributed between two schools were used to answer the first three questions. These were supplemented by interviews in which the individual children were asked set questions. In order to gain additional data on question 1 above children from grades one, three, and five of a third school were similarly questioned during interviews. This was done to prevent the study from being strictly limited to the third grade. This last school was chosen partly because there was no regular science instruction in the grades. Question 4 was studied exclusively by means of the interview questions.

During the classroom sessions, the children could be observed in situations which were more natural than was provided by the interviews. The interviews were included, however, to furnish some information which could be obtained under conditions which were relatively constant for each child.

Question 1. What sources of information do children tend to use or suggest in response to various types of problems and what are their attitudes toward such sources?

From the running records taken in the classroom it was found that third grade children use or suggest both empirical and authoritarian sources of information. There is no evidence of a general predominance of one type above the other.

It was found in connection with question 1 that the children's classroom remarks and actions concerning sources of information could be classified according to a set of five categories proposed by the investigator. In the case of empirical sources of information, a majority classification was made by asking five qualified teachers in addition to the investigator to arrange the children's statements in the five categories. The 74 examples of the suggestion or use of empirical sources of information and attitudes concerning empirical sources of information were divided among the five categories as follows:

1. Experiments with some measure of control—12 examples.
2. Experiments without the suggestion of a control—12 examples.
3. Manipulation of materials for the purpose of facilitating observation—2 examples.
4. Observation without manipulation but with or without the use of instruments—27 examples.
5. Attitudes concerning the use of empirical sources of information—21 examples.

Only those remarks which did not fit into any of the first four categories but which did fit into the fifth were included therein. Hence there were actually more expressions of attitudes about empirical sources than this classification indicates.

It can be seen that controlled experiments are relatively rare even among these children who have been accustomed to regular science classes weekly or oftener. Simple observation and visiting places for the purpose of observation are most common among the empirical sources of information suggested.

In addition, the 74 examples of empirical sources of information mentioned by the children were examined by four of the judges including the investigator for evidence of components of scientific method. The number of occurrences of each of these components is listed below. Only those examples which were considered as acceptable by three of the four judges were included.

1. Design of experiment or technique—14 examples.
2. Observation. Includes observation from personal experience—34 examples.
3. Theory or interpretation—7 examples.
4. Repetition or need of checking—11 examples.
5. Control—5 examples.

For the classification of suggestions and use of books and charts as sources of information, the investigator devised the following set of categories:

1. Suggestion that a specific book be consulted or the actual consultation of a specific book.
2. Suggestion that a specific type of book be consulted.
3. Suggestion that a book be consulted—neither book nor type of book specifically mentioned.
4. Book from which information is recalled specifically mentioned.
4. Information recalled from a book but book not specifically named.
6. Evidence of misreading a book.
7. Attitudes concerning the use of books.

The 75 examples available could be arranged according to this classification. The investigator and one other judge disagreed somewhat because of lack of precision in defining these categories, but the investigator did not consider it worth while to define the categories further.

Examples of the children's remarks which were put into the foregoing categories can be found on pages 23 ff.

It is evident that most suggestions for the use of books as a source of information were connected with the recall of information which the child realized would fit a certain problem. The name of the book was remembered in about half of such cases. When the first three categories are grouped together, it is seen that the suggestion that a book be consulted as a method of answering a problem occurred nearly every time the occasion was suited to it (see page 28). Recollection of past reading was mentioned more frequently, probably because the children observed were already well read on the subjects they were discussing in class. This can, perhaps, be taken as an indication that the science topics were well within the ability and interest ranges of the children.

The same children observed in the classrooms were asked a set of prepared questions during individual interviews. In these questions, the children were asked how they would find certain bits of information. There was a decided predominance of empirical suggestions in all the interviews. The relative predominance of the empirical over the authoritarian sources remained essentially the same in grades one, three, and five.

The question arises as to whether children dealing with questions appropriate to their level would be more influenced by the suitability or the accessibility of a source. This question is not answered altogether by this study, but some evidence is available in the comparison between the sources of information which children mentioned in the classroom and those suggested during the interviews. In the classroom, authoritarian sources were suggested as frequently as empirical sources, whereas in the interviews empirical sources were mentioned more frequently. The apparent discrepancy between the findings from the classroom records and from the interviews is perhaps explained by the fact that children making suggestions in the classroom do so from practical considerations. They are aware that they may be called upon to carry out their suggestions, whereas in an interview they do not expect to have to act on their suggestions.

The sources of information suggested in the classroom were largely suitable for the information required but accessibility was evidently a factor. There was a tendency for empirical sources to be mentioned when apparatus was at hand and for authoritarian sources to be mentioned when there was no apparatus near by. Although this relationship is not by any means proved in this study, it nevertheless is in agreement with the other findings.

In view of these findings, it is recommended that teachers be alert to provide opportunities for children to solve problems empirically. The children seem to recognize the appropriateness of such methods but probably get too little practice in using them. It may be desirable to bring simple apparatus into the room as a means of introducing this practice. It is recognized, of course, that in some problems children would do better to use authoritarian methods than to accept anything empirical. By practice and discussion children may become aware of the advantages and disadvantages of each of these methods so that they may have some basis for making their own choice. It may be that children can be taught to weigh the quality of the authorities that are available (in books, encyclopedias, by word of mouth, etc.) against their own skill or awkwardness in empirical techniques. In this connection it may be advisable to let children try a performance in which they are unskillful so that they can realize the important place that motor skill and attention to details often occupy in empirical technique. For example, in demonstrations that require a bottle to be filled with steam children are likely to be slow in covering the bottle. As a result too much steam escapes and too much air enters the bottle; hence the demonstration will not be a success.

The study also indicates that children may retain considerable knowledge of subject matter from a lesson in which sources of information are stressed. Eight children from one class were questioned individually about the subject matter of two representative lessons six weeks after each lesson had taken place. One of these lessons had involved the use of apparatus by the children and the other had consisted of a discussion without apparatus. Eight children from a second class were similarly questioned on two of their lessons. In only one lesson from one of these classes was the recall of subject matter by the children considered unsatisfactory by the investigator.

Question 2. What is the effect of the teacher as far as can be ascertained in determining children's selection of sources of information and attitudes concerning such sources?

There was some evidence of the influence of the frequency of the teacher's statements of scientific attitudes on the frequency of those of the children in her class. There was also a tendency for children during the interviews to emphasize the source of information emphasized by the teacher. Both these statements are based upon evidence that is inconclusive and should be interpreted only as suggestions for further research.

Notwithstanding the unreliability of the information on this question, it would seem desirable for teachers to keep in mind their influence over the children and to develop their own standards as to what habits and attitudes are valuable.

Question 3. What sex differences are evident in the children's suggestions of sources of information?

All the sources of information suggested in the classroom were mentioned by both boys and girls. Sixty-one per cent of the remarks concerning sources of information were made by boys and boys made considerably more of the extraneous remarks as well. In fact, it is possible that the boys suggested more sources of information simply because they spoke oftener than the girls. It is impossible to conclude from this study whether girls suggest sources of information less frequently than boys because they have fewer ideas or because they are more hesitant about speaking in the classroom.

As stated on page 7, the investigator's running records from classrooms are not reliable quantitatively because all the remarks were not recorded. However, the investigator can think of no factors which would produce a sex bias in the records.

The girls suggested 69 per cent of the experiments although

the boys mentioned the majority of all the other sources of information. The girls spoke in the classroom less than the boys but when they did speak they suggested empirical sources as often as authoritarian. The boys, on the other hand, suggested authoritarian sources oftener than empirical. The evidence for this seems to be highly significant statistically, but the data are subject to the many variables present in a classroom situation.

The sex differences observed in the classroom records were not corroborated by the interviews with the children. The interviews all agreed in exhibiting no significant sex differences.

Further study is needed before a satisfactory interpretation of this discrepancy can be made. The sex differences in the classroom may be of a relatively superficial nature and the findings from this part of the study must be treated accordingly.

Question 4. What is the relation between sources of information cited and difficulty of problem?

Question 4 points the way to further research as this study reveals a possible decrease in the tendency to suggest an empirical source of information rather than an authoritarian source with an increase in the difficulty of the question. The difficulty of the question was measured by the number of children who failed to answer it.

If this tendency should be established by further investigation, it would indicate an element of common sense on the part of children in selecting a source of information. Whether this common sense occurs in children without its being taught or not, teachers will wish to foster it. Making children conscious of their abilities and limitations is, perhaps, the most valuable contribution a teacher can make in helping them to learn to select sources of information for their questions and problems.

SUMMARY

In summary, this study indicates some of the uses children make of empirical and authoritarian sources of information. Both sources were used by both boys and girls under all the circumstances investigated. However, during the individual interviews there was a preponderance of empirical suggestions while during the classroom sessions authoritarian suggestions were made just as frequently. There is some evidence that the teacher may influence the children's choice of sources of information by her own remarks as well as by arranging apparatus for the children to use. It appears important for the teacher to have a good background in the uses of various sources of information and to possess a well worked out philosophy about the values and place of these sources so that she will be able to lead children in their handling of problem situations. No conclusive sex differences were found. It is possible that the difficulty of the problem with which a child is confronted may partially determine the sources of information he suggests for it, but this is indicated rather as a study worthy of further investigation than as a piece of conclusive evidence.

Further research should be carried out along the lines suggested by the last three questions investigated in this study. Answers to these questions are imperative in advising the classroom teacher properly as to how to develop the children's resources for answering problem situations in science.

At present there is a tendency on the part of some teachers to push the subject matter of the sciences lower in the grades. The wisdom of this procedure may be questioned from more than one point of view. The tendency, observed in this study, was for the source of information to change as the problem became more difficult. If this finding should be corroborated by further research, there would then be an additional basis for judgment on areas of subject matter suitable for different aged children.

Bibliography

ALPERT, AUGUSTA. *The Solving of Problem Situations by Preschool Children*. New York: Bureau of Publications, Teachers College, Columbia University, 1938.

COHEN, MORRIS and NAGLE, ERNEST. *An Introduction to Logic and Scientific Method*. New York: Harcourt, Brace, 1936.

CROWELL, VICTOR F. "The Scientific Method." *School Science and Mathematics*, XXXVII: 523-531, May 1937.

CURTIS, FRANCIS P. *Some Values Derived from Extensive Reading of General Science*. New York: Bureau of Publications, Teachers College, Columbia University, 1924.

DAVIS, IRA C. "Is This the Scientific Method?" *School Science and Mathematics*, XXXIV: 83-86, January 1934.

———. "Measurement of Scientific Attitudes." *Science Education*, XIX: 117-122, October 1935.

DEUTSCHE, J. M. *The Development of Children's Concepts of Causal Relationships*. Minneapolis: University of Minnesota Press, 1937.

DEWEY, JOHN. *Logic, The Theory of Inquiry*. New York: Henry Holt, 1938.

DOWNING, ELLIOT R. "Does Science Teach Scientific Thinking?" *Science Education*, XVII: 87-89, April 1933.

FISHER, R. A. *Statistical Methods for Research Workers*. London: Oliver and Boyd, 1936.

GANS, ROMA. *A Study of Critical Reading Comprehension in the Intermediate Grades*. New York: Bureau of Publications, Teachers College, Columbia University, 1940.

GEORGE, WILLIAM H. *Scientist in Action*. New York: Emerson, 1938.

HAUPT, GEORGE W. *An Experimental Application of a Philosophy of Science Teaching in an Elementary School*. New York: Bureau of Publications, Teachers College, Columbia University, 1935.

HOFF, A. G. "A Test for Scientific Attitude." *School Science and Mathematics*, XXXVI: 763-770, October 1936.

ISAACS, SUSAN S. *Intellectual Growth in Young Children*. New York: Harcourt, Brace, 1930.

71

KEYSER, CASSIUS. *Thinking about Thinking*. New York: Dutton, 1926.

LICHTENSTEIN, ARTHUR. "The Effect of Teaching Stress upon an Attitude." *Science Education*, XIX: 73-75, April 1935.

MONTAGUE, WILLIAM P. *Ways of Knowing*. New York: Macmillan, 1928.

NOLL, VICTOR H. "The Habit of Scientific Thinking." *Teachers College Record*, XXXV: 1-9, October 1933.

————. "Measuring Scientific Thinking." *Teachers College Record*, XXXV: 685-693, May 1934.

————. "Measuring the Scientific Attitude." *Journal of Abnormal and Social Psychology*, XXX: 145-154, July 1935.

————. "Teaching the Habit of Scientific Thinking." *Teachers College Record*, XXXV: 202-212, December 1933.

PEARSON, KARL. *Grammar of Science*. New York: Macmillan, 1911.

SKEWES, GEORGE F. "What Is a Scientific Attitude?" *School Science and Mathematics*, XXXIII: 964-968, December 1933.

UNDERHILL, ORRA E. *The Origins and Development of Elementary School Science*. Chicago: Scott, Foresman, 1941.

WELLER, FLORENCE. "Attitudes and Skills in Elementary Science." *Science Education*, XVII: 90-97, April 1933.

WEST, JOE YOUNG. *A Technique for Appraising Certain Observable Behavior of Children in Science in Elementary Schools*. New York: Bureau of Publications, Teachers College, Columbia University, 1937.

DATE